HOWARD AKLER

MEN OF ACTION

COACH HOUSE BOOKS, TORONTO

first edition

 Canada Council **Conseil des Arts**
for the Arts du Canada

 ONTARIO ARTS COUNCIL
CONSEIL DES ARTS DE L'ONTARIO
an Ontario government agency
un organisme du gouvernement de l'Ontario

Canada

Published with the generous assistance of the Canada Council for the Arts and the Ontario Arts Council. Coach House Books also gratefully acknowledges the support of the Government of Canada through the Canada Book Fund and the Government of Ontario through the Ontario Book Publishing Tax Credit.

LIBRARY AND ARCHIVES CANADA CATALOGUING IN PUBLICATION

Akler, Howard, 1969-, author
    Men of action / Howard Akler.

(Exploded views)
Issued in print and electronic formats.
ISBN 978-1-55245-317-9

    1. Akler, Howard, 1969-. 2. Consciousness. 3. Brain. I. Title.
II. Series: Exploded views

BF315.A42 2015   153   C2015-905030-8

Men of Action is available as an ebook: ISBN 978 1 77056 426 8.

This book is for Saul's family

1

The first time I shaved my father, he was in a coma. This most quotidian of tasks turned surreal: shook a can of Gillette Foamy, lathered his unresponsive face. I admit to nerves. He was, until the last difficult months at home, always well-groomed, and there was a clear obligation to keep him so. I thumbed his chin to the left. Began on the right. My initial stroke disturbed not a whisper – his skin was too slack – and it took repeated attempts before I was able to hold his cheek taut enough with one hand and angle the blade properly with the other.

With burgeoning barberish confidence I continued to chin and jaw and was a cool hand around the tracheostomy hole in his throat. This was a new intimacy with the old man. I felt for the first time his familiar dewlap. Paid close attention to the mole by his left ear; half-splattered with thick white foam, it reminded me then and since of a fire hydrant in a snow drift.

Such assiduity creates its own blindness. I rinsed the cheap plastic razor, tapped loose stray bristles. Only when I turned to appreciate my job did I notice I had left his sideburns long, like mine.

2

Assets and liabilities. He knew his way around a balance sheet. Saul was a chartered accountant for over five decades. The bulk of his clients were in the building trades – masonry, excavation – and he was well acquainted with all the necessary writeoffs. He liked to calculate depreciation in his head. He'd light a cigar, slowly, work it between thumb and forefinger for several silent seconds. It gave him time to think.

3

The second time I shaved my father I was conscious of several spots I'd missed before, those hard-to-reach areas common to many men: under a nostril, side of the lips. There was an entire thatch hidden in his labiomental crease.

Okay, I said into my father's unhearing ear. *Here we go*.

That morning, I had studied my own face in the mirror. Made note of the grooves and nooks that gave me depilatory trouble and tried, later, to transpose them.

As I wiped clean the residual blots of shaving cream, I was mortified to see I'd nicked him. Momentarily mortified. *The man's in a coma*, I said out loud. *Who gives a shit about a dot of blood on his chin?*

4

It has been fourteen months since he died, thirty since the surgery, and what lingers most is not the shock of the tumour, nor its sombre consequence, but all the sitting, the sedentary hours at his bedside while I tried to get my head around what had happened in *his* head. Because when he emerged from the coma he was not the same. His awareness was erratic. Brief coherent stretches were bookended by much lengthier ones in which he was muddled, mute. I would shift in my hard hospital chair and attempt to stay vigilant. Note any small sign of consciousness – a nod, a smile. The most important thing, during those long answerless days, was to simply pay attention.

5

It was my father, of course, who taught me to shave. I was a nominally hirsute teen and he was in his early fifties. How many father-son rituals would we share? He taught me to ride a bike. To skate. Driving would come later; a frank talk about sex never did.

I suspect I was happy to be initiated in this adult routine. We stood shirtless, side by side, lathered faces in the bathroom mirror.

6

Every few months I grow a beard. Or, to be more precise, I stop shaving. It is this lack of action that fosters growth.

7

'To pay attention,' writes the essayist Sven Birkerts, 'to *attend*. To be present, not merely in body – it is an action of the spirit. "Attend my words" means incline your spirit to my words. Heed them. A sentence is a track along which heeding is drawn.' He goes on to say the etymological background of the word *attend* is to stretch toward: 'Paying attention is striving toward, thus presupposing a prior wanting, an expectation … Reading, at those times when reading matters, we let the words condition an expectation and move toward it.'

8

His eyes were open the third time. Who knows what he saw? I looked at him and a vacant gaze looked back.

I lathered him up. From cheekbone to jowl, he seemed oblivious to each scrape of the blade. I shaved his neck and chin and tilted his head to tidy up the space under his nose. Then, while I searched out the inevitable strays, my father did a remarkable thing: he drew down his upper lip. He flattened his philtral dimple so I could properly shave that hard-to-reach spot. This tiny movement could have been conscious or merely a reflexive response to the touch of the razor on his face. I sat down. I bounced the possibilities around. Chin in hand, I waited for more.

9

For fifty-seven years, he sat at his desk and worked with numbers.

For twenty-three years, I've sat at my desk and worked with words.

The beauty of his profession: it all adds up.

10

I suffer from a lack of *sitzfleisch*, the ability to put my ass in a chair and keep it there until the day's writing is done. My first novel, a slender 160 pages, took eight years to write. The second will be almost as long, whenever it is finished. I put it aside two and a half years ago and applied all my sedentary determination to another chair.

The grief and uncertainty of a long bedside vigil is a sad match for my desperate need to shape and reshape sentences.

I can't help myself. I'm a born writer. By this I refer not to any rare insight nor special talent for sentences, but to a deep pathological need, noticeable from a young age, to rewrite my own history. It's an ontological state.

11

Nine to five, five days a week, fifty-two weeks a year (minus two for vacation) for fifty-seven years.

Adelaide, Temperance, Toronto streets. And then, finally, mimicking the migration of his generation's Jews, the firm pushed out of the cramped downtown core to north of the city's old border, at Steeles Avenue, into the suburban neighbourhood of Concord.

From where he would return home, every day, at 5:19 p.m.

It's a cliché, of course: the humdrum accountant, boring old bean-counter whose devotion to routine, to order, is evident both in and out of the office. Indeed, my father found tremendous comfort in sameness, an emotional stasis that required fidelity to the clock. Unburdened of briefcase and tie, he sat on the living room sofa at 5:30 and read the newspaper. Dinner at 6 – he neither cooked nor cleaned – and less than thirty minutes later was back in his car. He would not go anywhere. Only sat in the driveway and smoked a cigar. These were the times he was most actively alone; free from my mother's household business, from five-kid clatter, Saul could stay pungent and idle until he went back inside the house to watch television from 7 till 10:30, his bedtime.

For a man so wedded to certainty, it always seemed odd that he liked to gamble. Over the years, he played cards, lotteries and, most of all, the horses – though it should be noted, perhaps truer to his cautious nature, he only ever bet the two-dollar minimum.

The track and the office, the office and the track. These were the far-off places, places of an adultness so unlike the domestic sort familiar to me. I used to imagine him there, his humour. The way he liked to kibbitz. Just because the stakes were small does not mean they were insignificant.

I went with him once as an adult. He'd initially chafed at the idea – his habit for decades, once various cronies stopped, was to go solo – but with distinct pleasure he described in detail long-ago exactors, near misses.

I put ten bucks on a horse named Honest Accountant, who predictably finished with a view of the field.

'Never bet on an honest accountant,' my father said.

Also, perhaps, a little predictably.

12

He was, at the age of seventy-nine, still going to the office every day. He was driven, I suspect, by his need for routine, since he was not a man known especially for his dynamism. He was, however, known for his reliability, and this ultimately began to slip. Papers piled up on his office desk and the one at home. Simple returns took days not hours. Some he even filed late – a first for him – and his firm was forced to pay a penalty. His partners began to grouse, and it was decided he would retire on August 31, 2009.

His first client was a barber. His last client was a barber.

The question, to me, always baffles: *So, what do you do?* Casually intended, just a bit of small talk, I nonetheless hem and haw. To answer *writer* is to invoke not only the long stretches when I cannot write, when I cannot get the words to make sense on the page, but also the much, much longer stretches in which I earn little or nothing from my work. It speaks directly to my struggle to reconcile vocation and avocation.

Saul had no such dilemma. A proud professional, proud to support a family of seven, his question was not what do you do, but what do you do *now*? His retirement would redefine him. No longer a partner in a small but lucrative firm, not anymore a man who could enjoy the chit-chat with clients and colleagues, my father – who did not like change – would now face nothing but.

13

Truth is: 90 percent of my writing life is spent not writing. I open the notebook, blank page ablaze with possibility. This is the moment to pick my ear. Or stare out the window. I ruminate heroically. So driven to produce that I commit nothing to paper, clinging through the lost hours to all options. Only in the dying moments of the work day do I jot down three or four words, my clumsy scrawl like the blip of a heart monitor.

Part of the problem is my concentration is poor. I can't sit still. The click of a pen is a starter's pistol and I'm off, an adrenal lunatic, apace up and down the hallway. A nomad in my own home.

The more I wander, the less present I become: my emotional life is too connected to what I put or do not put on the page. When I cannot write, I lose my sense of self. I begin to disappear.

14

More than a year into his retirement, my mother began to call with weekly updates. She had the vantage point, after half a century of homemaking, to describe with worried precision the slow unravelling of his habits: he stayed up past midnight watching TV, he slept till 10:30 this morning, ate breakfast after noon, skipped lunch altogether.

Without work, the architecture of his days was altered irreparably. He had retained a few clients, small ones with simple accounts that he could handle at home, but he grew too unfocused, too forgetful. Deadlines escaped him completely.

The calls went from weekly to daily: he stays in his pyjamas all day, never leaves the house, just stares off into space.

The problems in his head were complicated by those that occurred in his body. Long-standing conditions with his heart and his colon lead to three hospitalizations in two years. The atrial fibrillation required a short stay but it was the flare-ups of colitis that really seemed to wear him down. He spent half his retirement on the toilet, the other half in front of the television.

15

'Books address the ear, a timeless organ. A movie imprisons your eyes. It acts on you, not you on it. Hence, you don't "see" or "look at" a movie. You *watch* it the way a cat watches a bird ... ' This from Leonard Michaels, a favourite of mine; his early short stories are breakneck, dirty, every word in them, as he once said, is alive to the other; his later essays are learned and agile; his lone screenplay a tremendous dud.

Pick just about any night of the past fifty years and Saul could be located in his chair in the den of my parents' North York bungalow. Watching TV. His devotion to the tube could be discerned by the imprint his body left behind on the seat cushion, his particular combination of weight and slouch, individual as a fingerprint. And like a fingerprint, as a clue to his former presence.

TV shows he liked: *Columbo*, *The Rockford Files*, *Agronsky & Company*, TV Ontario's *Saturday Night at the Movies*.

Actually, our most resonant father-son moments occurred on those Saturday nights, spread across the 1980s, when we watched old movies together. My teenaged eyes captured by the same black-and-white images that had captured *his* teenaged eyes forty years earlier.

This Gun for Hire, *Double Indemnity*, *The Reckless Moment*, *Force of Evil*, *Kiss of Death*, *The Glass Key*, *Caught*, *The Maltese Falcon*, *Out of the Past*.

Though he did not share the gosh-gee manner of the show's avuncular host, Elwy Yost, my father would display a previously unheard prosody when reminiscing about those long-ago screen baddies: Tommy Udo, Smith Ohlrig, Kasper Gutman.

He appreciated when an actor looked good in a suit, like William Powell.

And when he didn't, like Robert Mitchum.

He was especially fond of tough-guy actors who were born Jewish: Kirk Douglas (Issur Danielovitch), John Garfield (Jacob Julius Garfinkle) and Edward G. Robinson (Emanuel Goldenberg).

He was always quick to rah-rah Jewish achievement, so it should come as no surprise that he relished the performances of these men. They were not just Jews who made it big in Hollywood; they were Jews who rose from humble beginnings and remade themselves into pure cinematic manhood: snappy, savvy, no-nonsense.

'He liked to imply he had street smarts,' one of my father's former colleagues told me at the shiva. 'He wanted you to know that he knew the score.'

His father was once duped out of his share in a dry-cleaning business. This was 1939. The full facts are lost to history, but were they lost on my nine-year-old father? I remember him telling me this story with resignation. It sounds like cheap motivation, of course – a screenplay-thin line of reasoning. But still.

In his 1959 book, *The Presentation of Self in Everyday Life*, the sociologist Erving Goffman describes face-to-face interaction in dramaturgical terms. We all play a role, he writes, and within each performance is a tacit understanding of dialogue, gesture, dress. Everything we say and do and wear contributes to the creation of our character.

His old boss called him Mr. Akler; his young children called him Daddy; to his cousins at the card table, he was Such, a family nickname of uncertain origin (although he claimed it came from his mother, who always said he was *such* a nice boy). To each of these ears he would offer the appropriate lines of dialogue, say whatever was relevant to create his desired self.

If Emanuel Goldenberg could chomp on a cigar and spit out something phlegmatic, why not Saul Akler?

16

The word *self* condenses several complex notions into four small letters. There is the physical body embedded in a particular environment, with its vast attendant sensory impressions. Paradoxically, there is also the non-physical feeling, which incorporates such concepts as free will, temporal continuity and, most curiously, the ability to reflect. To see itself, to create and recreate it.

The philosopher Daniel Dennett considers the self as a narrative centre of gravity, a theorist's fiction. The centre of gravity is a commonly held abstraction that, in spite of its abstractness, is still essential to understand the physical world. 'In effect it averages over all the gravitational attractions between every particle of matter in a thing and every particle of matter on the planet, and tells us that we can boil all that down to two points – the centre of the earth (its centre of gravity) and the centre of the gravity of the thing – and calculate the behaviour of the thing under varying conditions ... What then is a centre of *narrative* gravity? It is also a theorist's fiction, posited in order to unify and make sense of an otherwise bafflingly complex collection of actions, utterances, fidgets, complaints, promises, and so forth, that make up a person. It is the organizer of the personal level of explanation.'

17

By no stretch of the imagination was he tough. I don't mean in the manner of mere fisticuffs, of course, but with regard to the more errant forms of emotional drama. I remember the day his cousin, deathly ill from skin cancer, called from the hospital to talk and my father cut him off to go watch an old movie on television. Ditto the time I dropped by to tell them I had broken up with a girlfriend. These were scenes that required no banter, nothing more than a genuine ear. He was a poor listener. He absented himself.

On the other hand, Saul was never more gloriously present than when he spoke of the past. This dichotomy drew me in; his grasping recollections were in a vivid modern voice. His stories from the 1940s and 50s landed black-and-white in my young ear: of Gotkin, who wanted to blow up the subway, of Appleby the womanizer and bookie. There was the one about the car ride with a cop, an old neighbourhood friend who carried a shotgun in the back seat. Someone pulled the trigger and blew a hole in the passenger door. I think it happened on Manning Avenue. I developed a nostalgia for his city: a pool room near Bellevue Avenue, a deli on Spadina. As a teenager, I biked down to Sunnyside Beach after he told me about the outdoor dance floor, the Sea Breeze, that used to be there.

My first novel is set in this era, on many of these same streets. I thought up Jews tough and glib, loose in a city new to skyscrapers, traffic woes, mass media.

Is it safe to say my interest in Toronto history, a gleeful immersion in the quasi-illicit, began somewhere in his mind?

18

More than anything he actually *did*, he told me what he watched. And where: the Alhambra Theatre, at Bathurst and Bloor Streets, with its Moorish arch above the marquee; and the art deco Pylon, on College.

Up until the 1960s, movie houses ran films continuously. Newspapers did not list show times, so people simply showed up at any point during the screening, took their seats and, in the dark, did enough mental editing to piece together a plot. And they remained seated, through closing credits, newsreel and cartoons, till the movie began again and they could watch up to the scene at which they arrived. Then they got up to leave.

Hence the old saying, no longer much in use: *This is where I came in.*

19

He became less and less present. Mid-task, he would pause and stare at the ceiling for twenty minutes. My mother veered from concern to exasperation and back; she had great difficulty getting him to go anywhere.

On the day I came to help herd him to his cardiologist, my father sat in a bedroom chair, holding his pants. Five minutes passed, ten. He stared out the window, but it was clear whatever he was watching was on the other side of the forehead.

'Dad?'

He did not hear me so I raised my voice.

'Dad!'

With a start, he dropped his pants. I picked them up. 'Dad? Do you need a hand?'

One of his mild smiles. 'No.'

Later, in the den, I had to ask.

'Wha?' he said. A Cagney caper was on AMC, volume high.

'I said: you seem to be lost in thought a lot these days. What're you thinking of?'

This time his smile was shy. I had never before seen a hint of shyness in him. 'I like to make up stories,' he said.

'Stories?'

'Like a mystery. And I'm the detective. Looking for clues.'

I raised an encouraging eyebrow like a scandal-sheet editor, thoughtfully rubbed my chin like a crusading DA.

20

He fell. Once a month for six months, he fell somewhere in the house. In the shower, by the bed, approaching the fridge. He listed to the left when he sat, braced himself on a wall when he stood. The million prior journeys he had made meant nothing; every step was now uncertain.

Still, he clung to the familiar. With one hand on the wall he felt his way from hall to kitchen. He flipped on the coffee maker. Buttered his toast.

Sometimes he jotted down important facts, useless tidbits, fading memories, before they would completely elude him. From a list on his desk, with my annotations in italics.

Tankhouse Ale: *my father was not a big beer drinker – a six-pack would last the whole summer – but he took note whenever something struck his palate. He tasted this local beer in a Pickering restaurant when he visited my sister and her sons. It was perhaps his last time there.*

Hearing Batteries #312: *his first response to any question was always 'Wha?' This was partly because he was so hard of hearing, but that tiny pause also gave him time to consider what he would say back. Two years before he died, he tested a hearing aid but soon abandoned it because he didn't like to hear himself breathing.*

Calamari: *likely from the same Pickering meal.*

Bruschetta: *see above*.

Affordable Housing: *one of his bugaboos, along with daycare, welfare and the metric system. Our politics were so far apart we simply steered clear of touchy matters. Save housing. I had been a part-time eviction prevention worker for several years, so it was not always possible to avoid topics such as rent subsidies or public housing.*

Greer Garson (Barber Brown): *Saul grew up on Grace Street, south of Harbord. One of his neighbours, a barber named Brown, had a beautiful daughter who resembled the actress Greer Garson. Though he could no longer remember her name, my father beamed when he recalled her face.*

Compression Socks: *the most common medication for colitis is a steroid called Prednisone, which alleviates bowel irritation but also causes the body to retain water. My father's skinny legs would swell up to cartoon size, so he wore these heavily elasticized stockings to exert pressure on the legs and improve the flow of fluids. Nurses came regularly to help him in and out of the socks.*

Sonny Langer: *a well-known North York caterer.*

His bruised skin was always changing colour: from purple to green to yellow.

We all assumed this was encroaching dementia, that his debilitation had gotten to the point where his home had become too perilous. My siblings and I discussed geriatric assessments. My mother, obdurate as they come, understood that she now needed more care than she could provide. For his safety, for her sanity, she took the unprecedented step of calling a family meeting.

I felt a Cleaving in my Mind –
As if my Brain had split –
I tried to match it – seam by seam –
But could not make them fit –

A sweltering Thursday in July, exhaust-pipe air. I rode the Don River bike route down to Cherry Beach, took a cooling dip in Lake Ontario. It was two days before our family meeting. I settled under tree shade to read Lyndall Gordon's biography of Emily Dickinson. It's a nifty bit of detective work: Gordon follows the trail backwards from the poet's famed seclusion and oft-mentioned-yet-unnamed sickness and finds compelling evidence for epilepsy. She relies not only on semantic clues – 'Throe' and 'Fit' and 'Convulsion' all appear repeatedly in her work – but also on nineteenth-century context, in which the illness was stigmatized, kept secret. Marriage for epileptics was discouraged, not just due to hereditary dread, but also because the excitement of the marital act might cause a fit. Epilepsy was illegal in some states; in others, sufferers were simply locked up in asylums. No wonder Emily kept herself hidden. Though enduring lore ascribes her reclusiveness to a failed love affair, I was completely struck by this neurological explanation. The poet herself would write that this 'bolt' into her 'Existence' had imparted some higher knowledge.

Ten years earlier, my own bolt. March 24, 2002. Unlike Emily, I saw no aura of presentiment, no millisecond of supreme consciousness. I was merely confused. When I woke up I was unable to choose between two sweaters so wore them both. I went astray on my usual walk to work. When I did arrive at the bookstore, I was unable to count out change. Could barely alphabetize. Dimly aware of its own impairment, my mind slowly unlettered.

So when my friend Sarah dropped in to ask about a title, she saw my distress and hustled me out.

She asked me something. Bought me lunch.

The menu made no sense.

She repeated her question.

I saw the answer in my head. It was a simple sentence constructed of common words. But that glimpse was all I got; meaning was lost. Without definition the sentence became weightless, separated word by word. I looked over my shoulder and watched each one float away.

What does it say about my mind that, as I write this, I can suddenly remember that the book Sarah wanted was a detective novel by Robert B. Parker?

In Emergency with the worst headache of my life. Someone was talking: Sarah. She told me I had a seizure in the street, another in the ambulance. Seems I was conscious and communicative much of the time, though I remembered nothing till that moment. Awareness inched back slowly. My tongue hurt. I attempted a single word.

'Seizure?'

'Two, actually.'

'Whoa,' I said.

Sarah nodded. 'Also,' she said, 'the paramedic hit on me.'

Two generalized tonic-clonic seizures in relatively quick succession. Each lasting no more than a minute. CT and MRI scans were normal, though EEG showed a genetically determined tendency to seize (primary generalized). Seizure begins in no specific 'area' of the brain. It occurs everywhere at once.

I felt a Funeral, in my Brain –

This was the line I was reading when my sister called to tell me the family meeting was off. Saul had fallen again, twice in the same day, and the second time he opened a gash in his head. My mother called 911.

'He was lucid,' Trudy told me. 'He made the paramedics wait twenty minutes while he sat on the toilet.'

'Guess that means he's okay,' I said.

He wasn't, of course.

From an email sent early the next morning by my brother, Ed:

'We spoke with the attending physician and based on the CT scan that was done, Dad has two tumours, one in the right side of his brain and one in his spinal canal ... '

22

Spread across my desk are three scans of Saul's brain. The first one was taken prior to his surgery. The tumour, to my eyes, takes up one-sixth of available space in the skull; it shoves outward from the right frontal lobe and squishes the rest of the brain into a new, unworkable shape.

The second scan came immediately after the operation. It is grainier than the first, more diffuse due to the amount of swelling and blood on the brain. The image is whitest in the area abandoned by the tumour.

The final scan shows no swelling. The brain has shifted back into place.

When I look at these photocopied scans now I see a damaged brain, an organ that once but no longer construed Saul Akler: his familiarity with tax code arcana, his arch-conservatism, his affinity for B-movie tough guys. I see a mind gone astray and another, mine, become more fixed.

23

Descartes believed in the pineal gland. The eight-millimetre nubbin was in a logical spot – between the two hemispheres of the brain – and unlike much cerebral matter appeared to be untwinned. This singularity suggested to him spiritual purpose, the meeting place for the physical body and the mind's non-physical essence. The small gland, wrote the seventeenth-century rationalist, was the 'seat of the soul.'

Jump ahead 250 years and Cartesian dualism – the notion that mind and brain are made of distinctly different stuff – had few adherents. Most theories of consciousness began with the grey matter, a materialist orthodoxy that must, according to Daniel Dennett, 'account for every mental phenomenon using the same physical principles, laws, and raw materials that suffice to explain radioactivity, continental drift, photosynthesis, reproduction, nutrition and growth.'

And yet, despite this modern certainty, a new, more sophisticated dualism emerged. Neuroscientists, who saw everything on a microscopic level, wanted to track the activity of the brain's eighty-five billion neurons. Follow the quadrillion synaptic connections that occur at every single moment. To them, the question was how all this electrochemical hubbub transformed into knowable sensory data. Philosophers of the mind, meanwhile, only had eyes for the big abstract picture. *Thought. Emotion.* Neuronal answers seemed insignificant.

Maybe this was simply a failure of language. Two entrenched sides, two ways of saying the same thing.

Paul and Patricia Churchland, husband-and-wife philosophers, were early advocates for a neuroscientific approach to the mind. That there is now a basic consensus between the disciplines is in part due to their efforts. Still, this is only the tiniest step forward. True understanding of consciousness, they argue, will only come when our advanced technology is met with a great conceptual leap, a more expansive way of thinking and speaking about ourselves.

From a 2007 *New Yorker* profile of the pair: 'Paul and Pat, realizing that the revolutionary neuroscience they dream of is still in its infancy, are nonetheless already preparing themselves for this future, making the appropriate adjustments in their everyday conversation. One afternoon recently, Paul says, he was home making dinner when Pat burst in the door, having come straight from a frustrating faculty meeting. 'She said, "Paul, don't speak to me, my serotonin levels have hit bottom, my brain is awash in glucocorticoids, my blood vessels are full of adrenaline, and if it wasn't for my endogenous opiates, I'd have driven the car into a tree on the way home. My dopamine levels need lifting. Pour me a Chardonnay, and I'll be down in minute."'

24

The seizures jangled my cerebral cortex; short-term, my perspicacity was shot. For three frustrating weeks, I'd lose my way in the middle of a sentence. The right word would perch on my tongue, pretty as you please, then suddenly alight for parts unknown.

It was stranger on the page. Comprehension was no problem but I retained very little of what I read. So I took notes. Copied out sections from Peter Whybrow's book on mood disorders, convoluted plot points of a Lew Archer mystery. But with the click of a pen my handwriting changed. My usual cryptic scrawl was displaced by the clarity of block letters. This was unplanned. 'Unconsciously,' Melville wrote in *Moby-Dick*, 'my chirography expands into placard capitals.'

One month later, without warning, those capitals returned to quiet cursive.

This cognitive impairment was brief, minor. Nothing but a small, weird hassle compared to more common troubles I have with mood. I've struggled with depression since my teens, lost enormous chunks of life to bleak lethargy. Most telling is my fluctuating relationship with language. During depressive episodes – short as a day, long as a year – anything I read, everything I write, lies desiccated on the page. Words so dried of meaning that it is impossible to believe they could ever express a single, simple thought.

And then it gets complicated.

Because even in the midst of so much nothingness, there are times when the sound and shape of letters begin to resonate. Syllables start to bounce and then to rhyme. Soon, my entire lexicon is alliterative. These moments, called clang associations, speak to a mild mania. They do not, however, make composition any easier; words suddenly drenched with awareness still rattle in a head full of rain.

We did have our family meeting that weekend, only it was held not at my parents' house but in a conference room at Sunnybrook Health Sciences Centre. The young neurosurgeon who presided, Dr. Phan, had good looks and bad posture. His simple, confident manner impressed my father.

According to the MRI, the tumours were likely noncancerous types called meningiomas, which grow not from brain tissue itself but from the three thin layers of tissue covering the brain and spinal cord known as the meninges.

The doctor told us the smaller tumour, behind the second cervical vertebra, was not a priority. The larger one, which pushed on the right frontal lobe of my father's brain, was of more immediate concern.

Saul, slumped leftward in a wheelchair, nodded.

This tumour had been growing a long time, up to ten years, and, as it grew, it put pressure on the brain. Pushed it out of position. Without intervention, this continual pressure could soon result in paralysis, or coma.

And since the tumour was too large to treat with radiation, the doctor recommended surgery as the best option. There were risks, of course, especially considering age and health: 1 to 2 percent chance of dying on the operating table; 5 to 10 percent of post-operative brain damage that never improves; 10 to 15 percent of post-operative brain damage that does improve. Overall, though, the success rate for this operation seemed to be over 80 percent.

I shifted in my chair, retreated into idiom. 'Those are good odds, Such.'

My father looked from me to the doctor.

'Mr. Akler, do you understand everything we've discussed?'

Saul straightened himself in his chair and said, with all the emphasis he could muster, 'Absolutely!'

26

(from my notebook, 2002, based on *A Mood Apart*, by Peter C. Whybrow)

BEHAVIOUR IS AN AMALGAM OF BIOLOGY AND EXPERIENCE

WE LIVE PARALLEL LIVES – ONE IN THE MIND, ONE IN OUR BODIES

OUR COHERENT IMAGE OF THE WORLD IS AN INTERACTIVE PROCESS BETWEEN THE BRAIN'S BIOLOGY AND OUR EXPERIENCE (MEMORY). BUT EACH ONE CAN CHANGE THE OTHER. EACH BRAIN EVOLVES ACCORDING TO EXPERIENCE, MOVES BEYOND ITS ORIGINAL GENETIC MAKEUP

TOO AWARE OF MY OWN SUBJECTIVITY

27

There was no foggy presage with the second pair of seizures, no language deficit thereafter. This was seven years after I was first struck, and what I remember most is not remembering, of being told afterward that my answers to the ER doctor's questions were two decades out of date:

- – I gave my boyhood address rather than my adult one.
- – I said I was a journalist despite the lack of an even remotely recent byline.
- – I did not recognize my girlfriend of seven years.

Short-term memory loss is a common post-seizure side effect, but I cannot square, to this day, the fact that I was awake but not fully aware, conversant for those two hours but caught in a past self.

28

July 16, 2012: heat alert, smog advisory, brain surgery. I'd already sweated through my shirt when word came that the operation would be delayed because of a botched hold-up at a Pickering veterinarian clinic; police had shot a seventeen-year-old male and he was on his way to Sunnybrook, the first available trauma centre.

The delay evinced no emotion from my father. He had, over the years, professed little in the way of introspection, and I like to think this served him well during those most uncertain of hours. He chatted, dozed, perhaps lolled in one of his tough-guy daydreams.

Or am I too eager to ascribe to him some form of fedoraed fatalism? I remember all too well that horrible moment, over twelve hours later, when the hospital attendants finally wheeled him away and his words rose a panicked octave: *Pray for me*.

The first reference to a meningioma-like tumour is found in the case report by Felix Plater, Professor of Medicine at the University of Basel, in 1614. His patient, Caspar Bonecurtius, 'a noble knight, began to lose his mind gradually over a two year period, to such an extent that he finally was completely stupefied and did nothing rationally.' After Bonecurtius died, Plater's autopsy revealed a 'round fleshy tumour like an acorn. It was hard and full of holes and was as large as a medium-sized apple. It was covered with its own membrane and was entwined with veins. However, it was free of all connections with the matter of the brain, so much so that when it was removed by hand, it left behind a remarkable cavity.'

There followed a period of more than 220 years when surgeons unsuccessfully attempted to remove a meningioma. 1743: Lawrence Heister, in Germany, operated on a thirty-four-year-old Prussian soldier and applied a caustic of lime. The soldier developed a post-operative infection and died. 1768: Olaf Acrel, in Sweden, explored a lesion with his finger and triggered a severe hemorrhage and delayed seizures which killed his patient days later.

But on July 29, 1835, Zanobi Pecchioli, Professor of Surgery and Operating Medicine at the University of Siena, operated on a forty-three-year-old with a fungating mass at the right sinciput. Pecchioli drilled three burr holes and removed a triangle of bone from the skull. He resected the tumour and covered the operative site with cambric covered in almond oil.

The patient recovered.

And when the Glaswegian surgeon William Macewan, who had previously been mocked for his progressive ideas such as an insistence on wearing a sterilized surgical gown, completed another successful resection on July 27, 1879, the modern era of meningioma treatment had begun.

It was exquisite, excruciating work. Mortality rates, even in the early years of the twentieth century, were barely 50 percent. 'The two major problems,' according to historian Michael Bliss, 'were bleeding and bulging. From the moment a surgeon cut into a patient's shaved scalp he had to deal with highly and delicately vascularized regions of the body. It got worse when he got through the skull (even bone can ooze blood) and opened the meninges, the three membranes – dura, arachnoid, and pia mater – that envelop the brain. The vessels saturating the meninges, surface, and tissues of the brain bleed easily ... surgeons often had to retreat from a bloody mess without achieving anything. They would be lucky to get out without causing the patient to bleed to death.'

An even more gruesome complication could occur once the surgeon had created a hole in the patient's head. The release of intercranial pressure could 'cause portions of the brain to bulge or herniate through your opening, and you could not get them back in again. Sometimes you could not close the dura after an operation. After 1890 most of the best operators followed Wilhelm Wagner in making a bone "flap" by connecting their drill or trephine holes, which they would fold back using the scalp as a hinge. But with bulging they could not close the flap. When brain tissue herniated, it soon became infected, creating a dreaded "fungus cerebri," and the patient soon died.'

American surgeon Harvey Cushing collated advancements in anesthesia, antisepsis and diagnostics in order to develop the best practices for the nascent field of neurosurgery. In 1904, according to Bliss, he wrote a 'major but still tentative "apologia"' about this procedure; two years later, he began to publish virtual 'how-to manuals for brain work.' And then in 1910, his successful surgery on the country's top military general, Leonard Wood, made him a world-renowned specialist.

Cushing coined the term *meningioma*, after the three layers of membrane that cover the central nervous system, in 1922. In 1938, along with Louise Eisenstadt, he issued the comprehensive monograph *Meningiomas: Their Classification, Regional Behavior, Life History and Surgical End Results*. At 741 pages, it was a noteworthy document; more impressive was that he had reduced the mortality rate below 10 percent.

Again, Bliss: 'In the first decade of the twentieth century, Harvey Cushing became the father of effective neurosurgery. Ineffective neurosurgery had many fathers.'

Even now I'm startled out of my solipsism: ours was not the only drama that night. There was another family ahead of us in the surgical waiting room, a couple hunched together on a couch. I recall little, if anything, of them. Sunburned knees? Cargo shorts? Mostly I remember my resentment that these people had intruded upon our anxious chitchat, our dubious silences, our nervous regurgitation of scant neuro-surgical knowledge.

An endotracheal tube was inserted. The incision site, on his right upper forehead, was shaved, sterilized, then injected with a localized anesthetic and a shot of adrenaline.

We had the numbers – there was my girlfriend, Susan, and myself, plus my mother, Nonni, and two of my brothers, Matt and Ed, who was accompanied first by his father-in-law, then by his wife. We took over the room. Swapped an uneven exchange of diagnoses, platitudes with that other family. I stayed silent and fixed my eyes on the wall-mounted television where CP24, the local news loop, screened the city apace: traffic snarls, mayoral antics, Blue Jays losses. I shifted my weight. The sunburned couple escaped. I watched for a second time the segment on weather, a week-long heat alert grown surreal since twelve straight hours of hospital air conditioning had left me with permanent goosebumps.

A curved incision was made on the scalp and then the skin was peeled back to reveal the skull.

Surgical reports are written in the passive voice. The operative hand is always being *placed* somewhere. Orwell, in his essay

'Politics and the English Language,' suggests that the passive voice obscures blame, avoids responsibility, as if there were some external force at work. But that notion is turned on its head when writing about an operation. The passive voice requires objectivity because only sober rational scientific method can be trusted.

Me, I wanted anything *but* sobriety. *I* fidgeted in my chair. *I* paced the hospital corridor.

A cranial perforator was used to drill a series of small burr holes in the skull, each nickel-sized in diameter. A surgical saw was used to connect the holes and the bone flap was created. There was now a window in Saul's skull.

Less than two hours into the operation, the hospital's public address system blurted alert: Code Orange.

We shrugged among ourselves. Code Red, everyone knew, indicated fire. Code Blue was for cardiac arrest. No one had any inkling about Code Orange.

The first ambulance arrived just before 11 p.m. Five more followed within the hour. We heard the chaotic footfalls of police, paramedics, reporters. The news was outside the waiting room before it hit the television screen above our heads. CP24 reported gunfire at a block BBQ party on Scarborough's Danzig Street. The initial report said over twenty people had been shot.

Code Orange, we learned, was the call for mass casualties.

The head ER nurse was on the red phone with EMS dispatch in an attempt to clarify which gunshot victims were going where. Cellphones went off all over the place. Not just doctors, nurses and residents but also CT scan technicians, security, cleaning staff. I imagine them all, amped up, uncertain, ready to go, while the six most critically wounded were carefully settled into the trauma bays.

One floor up, twelve eyes followed the story, now in its third loop. Updates were slow. Two people were now confirmed dead. The CP24 reporter struggled to find anyone able to parse the atrocity: music, booze, heat, bang-bang-bang. We turned away from the television and there was Dr. Phan.

I remember chewing my lip. Calculating hours: there was no way the operation was over.

In fact, the operation was on hold. Dr. Phan said there were concerns that the sheer number of casualties could deplete the blood bank supply and there would be nothing available if – and here he stressed *if* – Saul was in need of a transfusion. Otherwise, it was going well. We heard that the bone flap had been created. We were assured that there would likely be no complications from an extended anesthetization. We were told to be patient. Nobody knew how long this would take; there had never been a Code Orange at Sunnybrook before.

'I should get back to Saul,' Dr. Phan said, and then he paused as if to gauge the credulity of what he was to say next. 'Because, you know, he has a hole in his head.'

31

Wilder Penfield was Cushing's most famous student. He performed hundreds of successful operations during his surgical career and founded the Montreal Neurological Institute in 1934. He specialized in the treatment of severe epilepsy.

The brain may be an elaborate processor of sensory data, but it is itself without sensation. So, Penfield and his longtime collaborator Herbert Jasper used only local anesthetic. Their patients were fully conscious and able to answer questions as the surgeons slowly moved an electrode across the folds and contortions of their cerebral cortices.

Zap. 'Anything?'

'My tongue feels numb,' said one young woman.

Zap.

'A ... A ... A,' she vocalized.

A dozen verbal and reflexive responses later and Penfield had not only located the damaged tissue but also deduced how much was essential and how much could be removed with no detectable functional loss. He isolated the point of irritation – often a scar – that triggered a seizure and then excised it, confident there would be little risk of paralysis or aphasia.

In this way, he mapped the brain's centres for speech and movement, a cartography still current.

He was a pioneer in neurophysiology and neurosurgery. But Penfield struggled with his strangest discovery. Stimulation of the temporal lobe often set free a patient's long-dormant memory. The recollection described in vivid detail: a song once heard, verse and chorus expertly hummed years later; the fusty stink of a father's cigar. The kicker was that each patient, while immersed in ardent past, was also fully present. Every one of them aware of the surgical theatre, of the operating table and the inescapable fact that these flashes of memory were imposed upon them.

Penfield called this a 'double consciousness.' It confounded him. Here was a part of subjective experience he could not materially manipulate. Long an avowed man of science, he had no choice but to believe that the mind and the brain were not one thing, but two. He became a late-life dualist. His quaint but requalified analogy: 'There is a switchboard operator as well as a switchboard.'

32

And so we waited: waited through the early morning hours for the chaos of the trauma centre to subside, waited for the blood bank supply to be confirmed, for updates on the shootings, for the surgery to restart, for it to finish.

Time shook loose from the clock, freed itself from the artificial imposition of seconds, minutes, hours. A single moment endured beyond all possible physical law, then repeated itself. Matt went for a walk.

CP24 continued with coverage of the Scarborough shooting; looped segments showed the same blinking police cruiser, the same taped-off crime scene. The announcer retold the same spotty facts so often – one hundred in attendance, over twenty shot, two dead – that any new piece of information, however minimal, took on tremendous temporal significance. A short interview with a bystander stretched out far too long in my ear. The photo of fourteen-year-old murder victim Shyanne Charles took forever to see.

One year later, I came across a magazine profile of the neuro-scientist David Eagleman, who was quoted as saying, 'Time is this rubbery thing. It stretches out when you really turn your brain resources on, and when you say, "Oh, I got this, everything is as expected," it shrinks up.'

The writer of the profile is treated to an optical illusion, called the oddball effect, in Eagleman's lab: pictures of a plain brown shoe flashed over and over on a computer screen. Once in a while, a flower would appear instead. The writer believed that the flower stayed onscreen much longer than the shoe. But in reality, all the pictures remained onscreen for the same length of time. The only difference was the degree of attention the writer paid to them. 'The shoe, by its third or fourth appearance, barely made an impression. The flower, more rare, lingered and blossomed … '

Police officers and Susan and ER staff lined up at the Second Cup, the only kiosk in the hospital's food court to remain open all night. One cop, who had been at the scene, said there were no ambulance drivers available so he was ordered to take the wheel. In the confusion, he left his patrol car at the scene, locked and with the engine running.

At the front of the line, a woman dawdled and asked the countergirl, 'What can you tell me about those muffins?'

My mother retold the birth story of my father's baby sister, Cassy. Saul and his brother Nady were at the movies when she was born, and my grandfather had to drag them out of the theatre so they could meet her. They did their filial duty, then ducked out as soon as possible to catch the rest of the picture.

This is where I came in.

The final tally was twenty-seven victims: two dead, twenty-five shot, including a twenty-two-month-old baby who had been grazed by a bullet. One person had been trampled. The same clip of Police Chief Bill Blair continued to appear onscreen: 'In my thirty-five years of policing … '

I turned off the TV.

And then the rest of the night, or perhaps only my recollection of it, snapped forward: hubbub eased outside the waiting room, police came and went, Susan tried to knit, police went and came, Ed and I played a version of the alphabet game using only the names of obscure comic-book characters from our youth. 'Animal-Vegetable-Mineral Man,' he said. 'B'wana Beast,' I replied. A woman in scrubs passed by the door and bit into a danish. My sister, Trudy, arrived with her twelve-year-old son, police went, and when Dr. Phan reappeared to tell us the surgery was finally over, my mother stood up and applauded.

I keep coming back to Sven Birkerts. In an interview with the *Los Angeles Review of Books*, he breaks down the fundamental difference between fiction and nonfiction, a distinction more subtle and perplexing than the standard *did-it-really-happen?* criterion:

'Both processes are determined significantly by the sensibility, the psychological character, of the writer, but the actions mark the difference between essentially opposite kinds of agency. Fiction says 'let it be the case that' and nonfiction says, in whatever uniquely subjective way, 'it is the case that.' In fiction we must contend with the author's intention first and foremost: why this version of things? In nonfiction we must contend with the merger of the author's actual psyche and the actual world, and ask not so much why this version of things, as *how*? How did this account arise from this person, these givens?'

34

Saul was transferred to a post-operative recovery bed. We moved too; for six more hours we waited in a different room, bigger, with a formidable selection of age-old *Maclean's* magazine and a shifting contingent of families. Each one all ears. The moment the volunteer attendant announced a patient's name, one group or another would search out whichever floor, whichever wing, now held their loved one.

'Singh,' said the attendant, and then, an hour and a half later, 'Carpenter.'

The room emptied, refilled.

I was overcaffeinated, underslept and lost every game of movie Hangman to my twelve-year-old nephew. I guessed only four correct letters for *Diabolique* and three for *Rashomon* while he solved *The Major and the Minor* in less time than it took for me to write out the empty dashes of the movie's title.

'Akler,' said the attendant.

Fifth floor, D wing, room 24. His convalescence began well. He had a thick bandage on his forehead but far less facial swelling than I'd expected. He was able to state his full name, albeit drowsily, and even had tiny sips of soup and milk.

We were reassured enough, by mid-afternoon, to leave the hospital. I'd been awake for almost thirty-five hours. When I leaned close to say goodnight to my father, I nearly knocked the Foley bag loose from his bed.

He was drowsier the second day. Dr. Phan said the CT scan showed normal post-operative swelling and bleeding around the brain. Saul had trouble swallowing; he coughed himself awake. Eyes open, he gave us a weak wave. He asked for ice cream.

He was difficult to rouse all through the third day. I was at work and came by in the evening. Happily, he was at his most alert.

'Hi, Howie,' he said.

I told him he looked like John Garfield in *Body and Soul*.

The fourth day after his operation, July 20, he did not open his eyes nor did he respond to anyone's voice. The most recent CT scan showed no change in the amount of bleeding and swelling on the brain, but a blood test revealed a bladder infection. Was this enough to cause the setback? This possibility was quickly trumped by the EEG results, which determined Saul had been having non-convulsive seizures throughout the day. His breathing grew troubled, so he was transferred once again to the Critical Care Unit (CrCU), second floor, M wing.

This all happened when I was at work. It was a slow day on the eviction prevention desk, and when Susan called from the hospital, my mind couldn't keep up with her words. She had to repeat herself three times.

'So, he's conscious?' I asked.

'No. They sedated him.'

'Uh-huh.'

'He got agitated when they intubated him.'

'Okay.'

'They said that's a good sign.'

There are twenty beds in the Critical Care Unit at Sunnybrook. Neuro and trauma patients only. Because of the elaborate and delicate nature of the care involved, visitors are restricted to two at a time. I gave my name to the attendant behind a glass partition, who called a nurse inside the unit, who spoke to my father's nurse, who gave the okay, and two minutes later, I was buzzed in.

He was hooked up to more tubes and wires than on D5. I recognized the CVP line, the IV catheter, but little else. There were two monitors above his head rather than one. The biggest difference, certainly the most dire, was the ventilator. I watched Saul's chest rise and fall. A nurse, dedicated only to him, sat at the foot of the bed and logged data around the clock. My mother was by his side.

She said the plan was to keep him under sedation long enough for the Dilantin, an anti-convulsant, to build up to therapeutic levels in his system. The seizures had to be controlled so his brain could continue to recover. And then, in perhaps a few days, the doctors would ease him off the sedation and see how he responded.

I nodded.

An EEG technician slipped past me. Studied a monitor. I wondered which electronic beep represented Saul's brain.

I keep two notebooks. All my early drafts are handwritten. At home, I rely on the 300-page Selectum, spacious enough at 15.2 × 22.9 cm for each sentence to take its first breath.

Out of the house I always carry a Mead memo book. Pocket-sized at 12.7 × 7.6 cm, it is perfect for idle moments – at the coffee shop, on long subway rides, in libraries – places where I can work over the original sentences, loosen their knots until each one is limber enough to connect to the next:

Actually, if there was one father-son ritual we shared, it would have to be those weekend evenings when we watched old movies together.

Actually, the father-son ritual that reigns in memory is a montage of all those weekend evenings when we watched old movies together.

Actually, our most meaningful father-son ritual was centred on that show; what reigns is memory is a montage of all the old movies we watched together and the interviews conducted by the mustachioed, avuncular, perpetually awestruck host, Elwy Yost.

Actually, our most resonant father-son ritual occurred on those Saturday evenings, spread across the 1980s, in which my teenaged eyes were fixed on the same images, the same scenes, that had captured his teenaged eyes.

And so on.

Sometimes I read a particularly great sentence from another writer and stick it in there, such as the opening line from James Schuyler's poem 'Pastime':

I pick up a loaded pen and twiddle it.

This usage began to shift during Saul's time in the CRCU. Rather than fuss over revisions, I kept my pen clicked in order to record the sheer amount of medical information to come: doses of Lorazepam, Coumadin, Dilantin; names of critical care doctors; which test results confirmed which suspicions, and when he was scheduled for more.

And yet page after page in my old Mead memos show nothing of the sort. The first reference to my father's situation reads simply: *coma fart.*

I remember this. Remember that I was at his bedside, no other family there. The nurse had stepped away and then Saul farted.

I stood up. Searched for the nurse. I was, in those early days, obsessed with the distinction between reflexive and conscious action. Did a response – a twitch, a turn of the head – mean he was aware of his surroundings? I sat back down. He was being fed Resource, a liquid meal, through a tube. He would likely have some digestive burbles, conscious or not. I felt dumb. I wrote it down.

During this time, I should add, Susan kept detailed notes. A longtime keeper of notebooks herself, with many on the go to multiple ends, hers is the most objective record I have for what happened over the next year and a half.

Saturday, July 21: Saul had two visible convulsive seizures on his right side. He has a fever and the nurse took a culture sample to find out whether he has an infection or not. He has involuntary movement and reacts to stimulus when they test him. Evening's news was he's supposed to have another CT scan.

Sunday, July 22: Doctor said the anticonvulsant should be up to therapeutic levels. They'll take him off sedation tomorrow and do an EEG to see if there are more seizures. Saul's fever was gone today. He didn't have a CT scan yesterday or today. Someone said the blood on the brain is an irritant that is likely (or definitely?) causing the seizures.

Monday, July 23: Ed was here last night and got opposite information about the sedation. We think Saul was still under sedation during today's EEG, which showed more seizure activity, although smaller than the previous ones. Staff discovered a blockage in his feeding tube; a scope procedure showed it was some congealed liquid food and they removed it. He is now on three different anti-seizure medications. He is also on a steroid to help reduce swelling on his brain but it makes his hands swell up instead.

37

My oldest brother, Daniel, had flown in from Rishikesh, India. He brought a blanket to the hospital. We spread it out on a small patch of Sunnybrook grass and stretched out under a heavy sun.

'They're pretty careful with what they tell us,' I said.

'Hm-mm.'

'No one's called it a coma yet.'

His eyelids began to drop. Jetlag.

I continued: 'They talk about being awake. About being aware.'

Awareness, to my brother, was not a matter of knowing your name and occupation. It was a state of attention achieved after years of disciplined practice. It was a moment of pure consciousness, both simplified and heightened. Daniel had devoted much of the past decade to his pursuit of Eastern wisdom.

'How's Mom?' he asked.

'Okay,' I said. I knew she carried my father's wedding ring in her purse; in another pocket was his Do Not Resuscitate form. My mother had power of attorney for his personal care and had told me that, if the need arose, my father wanted doctors to do everything they could to keep him alive, but he did not want to be a vegetable.

This choice of words became more and more ominous the longer he remained in his current state.

Whatever that was.

38

Tuesday, July 24: Saul was slowly weaned off all sedation throughout the day. He began to have some slight eye movement, some coughing and gagging, which doctors say is involuntary movement but still a positive sign. His bandage has been removed and the bruise on his head is now visible. He has another CT scan this evening.

Wednesday, July 25: CT scan showed same amount of bleeding and swelling. Saul still on ventilator but he's breathing mostly on his own. Same involuntary movements as yesterday. Some concern about a blood clot in his leg, from being immobile so long. Nurse put anti-embolism stockings on him and will also start him on a blood thinner. He is supposed to have an EEG today.

Thursday, July 26: No EEG yesterday but they did one today. No results yet. Some concern that his right arm and hand are more swollen than his left so they'll do an ultrasound to check for possible blood clots. Same involuntary movements but he has not woken up. One CICU doctor said it could be a week before he wakes up; after that, they will have to consider what to do next. We've realized that different staff members have told us different things or one of the family members has information that contradicts another: today, for example, we learned he has been on two anti-seizure meds and not three. Also, he might not have had an EEG today.

39

'Actually, *coma* is a very subjective term,' one doctor told me amid the beep and buzz of the CICU. 'Every damaged brain will react differently.' She began to explain noxious stimulation, discussed decerebrate posturing, but this only made my own head beep and buzz. No one knew why he had gone downhill, so any confirmation, even the grim certainty of the word *coma*, would have been welcome.

That night, I Googled the Glasgow Coma Scale. Devised by Scottish neuroscientists for an efficient assessment of a patient's conscious state, the scale is used by emergency medical services worldwide. A patient who exhibits limited or altered consciousness is scored on four responses: Eye (1–not open to 4–open spontaneously), Verbal (1–non to 5–oriented) and Motor (1–none to 6–obeys commands) responses. The highest possible score, for a healthy and conscious person, is E4V5M6=GCS15.

My admittedly non-professional calculation for my father: E1V1M2=GCS4.

Objectively speaking, he was in a coma.

40

The brain is a three-pound lump with the consistency of soft tofu. It is also the most complex processor of information ever known. From the eyes alone, it receives one hundred billion signals each second. This data is assessed, sorted and disseminated along a network of eighty-five billion neurons, yet so densely interconnected that any one cell can reach another in seven steps or less. This baffles all computational models. Any overarching system, if one indeed exists, is far beyond our current comprehension.

But let's say we figure it out. Let's say, after decades of research and gazillions of dollars, scientists can successfully track the activity of every single neuron, every mechanism of cognition. Philosopher David Chalmers calls this the easy problem of consciousness.

The hard problem: how does the brain move beyond mere data processing to become subjectively aware of its own information?

It doesn't, according to Michael Graziano, professor of psychology and neuroscience at Princeton University. There *are* no subjective impressions, he writes. Only information in a data-processing device: 'When we introspect and seem to find that ghostly thing – awareness, consciousness, the way green looks or pain feels – our cognitive machinery is accessing internal models and those models are providing information that is wrong. The machinery is computing an elaborate story about a magical-seeming property. And there is no way for the brain to determine through introspection that the story is wrong, because introspection always accesses the same incorrect information.'

His theory rests on the difference between attention and awareness. The brain receives so much raw data it conserves computing resources by enhancing some incoming signals at the expense of others. This is the mechanistic process of attention. Awareness is the rough model, a simple reconstruction of that attention that allows us to focus our reason and behaviour and allows us to make our way through the world.

So the problem of consciousness may just be a semantic one. The brain absorbs a sea of sensory input, the tiniest fraction of which reaches the shore of our awareness. We pay attention to what is most novel, most necessary at the time. At its most reductive, the word *consciousness* refers to the synchronized firing of neurons across multiple areas of the brain, the mental experience of *attending*.

But should consciousness be summed up simply by its subconscious mechanism? I would prefer a more imaginative answer to the hard problem.

41

Consciousness, Graziano says, is the story our brain tells us.

This is the story I want to tell about consciousness.

42

Now and then I pause, shake the strangeness out of my pen: the Saul Akler in these pages is not Saul Akler, born April 27, 1930 – died November 06, 2013. Not exactly. Memory conflates, creates. I'm quite conscious of my mimetic task, of one mind that attempts to capture another mind on paper.

The question, of course, is this: did I *ever* really know what he thought?

Humans have the ability to ascribe mental states to others, a skill that most likely begins with an interior awareness – a sense of one's own intent, desire, even inclination to falsity – that is then applied to everyone we meet. This is a deeply creative act. Because we have direct access only to our own minds, we must rely on not just observation and inference but also great leaps of imagination in order to explain and predict the behaviour of others. Cognitive psychologists call this Theory of Mind and it means that our success as a species is dependent on how well we can read each other.

Observe, infer, imagine.

He took his morning blood-pressure medication with orange juice. Always three sips, his left hand always on his hip. He patronized the same steak house every birthday. He was a nervous driver. His usual car was a sedan but for the brief period in his early fifties when he owned a sporty Ford Cougar; it was blue, with bucket seats and not enough space to fit the whole family. He was big on small talk. Would chat up sales clerks, wait staff and then guess – most often correctly! – where each was born. He shrugged off difficult emotion, save for a constant ire at the socialists in City Hall. Otherwise, he *appeared* easygoing.

Passive by nature, he preferred to muffle himself inside a great calm. He avoided the unfamiliar rather than approach with curiosity. To be uncertain was to seem vulnerable. When in doubt, retreat to the television.

In the movies of my father's generation, a man gets socked in the jaw and hits the floor. He's back up in moments, maybe has a shot of whisky to clear his head. Is this a clue to interior life? Unable to articulate his own fears and disappointments, perhaps Saul experienced dark emotion as nothing more than a glancing blow.

43

Again: he made no claim on introspection.

And I, who have been lost time and again under the strata of self, have always found this hard to imagine.

44

Friday, July 27: CT scan showed no change. One CICU doctor explained that Saul is pretty much breathing on his own; at this point, the ventilator only suctions out saliva. Since there is a risk of pneumonia or vocal-cord damage if he is on ventilator for too long, they will perform a tracheostomy soon.

Saturday, July 28: No big changes. One nurse said it could take months for the swelling on his brain to decrease. We watched Saul yawn. His hair is growing back on the spot that was shaved.

45

Meanwhile, my own notes stretched further into the subjective. Whatever the day's complications, I continued to jot down only peripheral detail: *eyelashes.*

I had never noticed that his eyelashes were so long and thick. One of the nurses did; she often joked about how jealous she was.

More than his lashes, though, there was his strangely unlined face. His hair, though long receded, was not slicked down as usual with Brylcreem; it had regained some of its natural buoyancy. Really, despite the ugly purple bruise on his forehead and the presence of the respirator, I began to see my father as a much younger man.

A person rarely remains in a coma. Recovery, if it occurs at all, is a gradual process that can begin with the tiniest of movements, like the opening of an eye.

It's the opening and closing of the eyes, in fact, that distinguishes another disorder of consciousness, the vegetative state, from the coma. Vegetative patients return to sleep-wake cycles, and this was long assumed to be the limit of their experience. They were awake but not aware, lacking any of the higher cognitive functions associated with consciousness.

A more nuanced view has developed over the past decade, aided in part by tremendous advances in diagnostic technology. Much has been written on the pioneering work of British neuroscientist Adrian Owen, whose use of functional magnetic resonance imaging (fMRI) has helped to identify blips of cognition in otherwise unconscious people.

In 2006, Owen and his team attempted to communicate with a twenty-three-year-old woman in a persistent vegetative state. She was placed in an fMRI scanner, which tracks neural activity based on the increase of blood flow to a particular area of the brain. According to *Discover* magazine, Owen 'asked her to imagine one of two scenes – playing tennis or walking around her house – for thirty-second intervals ... In a normal brain, imagining tennis activates the supplementary motor area of the cortex, and picturing one's home prompts activity in regions involved in spatial perception, such as the posterior parietal cortex. This patient's brain responded exactly the same way.'

This type of mind reading caused quite a bit of hoopla in the mainstream press but also much tempered enthusiasm. Critics called fMRI a blunt instrument, incapable of isolating the action of a single neuron, let alone the interaction of billions needed to form a conscious thought. A digital representation of neural activity in one part of the brain, they cautioned, does not indicate individual experience.

What intrigues me here is the neural activity of the imagination. Not only can a brain, be it healthy or damaged, create and re-create images, it does so with incredible veracity. In fact, 'real' and 'fictional' stimuli follow similar causal pathways, achieve similar emotional effects. I can picture myself eating an apple and taste very close to an actual bite. I can read a book and respond to people on the page as if they were seated across the table.

47

By the end of July, Saul's EEGs showed no trace of seizures. My mother and I talked with several resident doctors who said they did not believe the blood and swelling on his brain was enough to cause a coma. The word *coma* pinged loud enough in my ear that I heard nothing of their description of a peripherally inserted central catheter (PICC). My mother repeated what doctors had just told us: Saul needed a long-term IV line because his arms were so swollen that staff have had trouble finding a vein.

The next day, Dr. Phan said Saul's eyes might have flicked open, might have tracked the movement of a penlight. He told us that the swelling on the brain had gone down and, as best as he could tell, there was no irreversible brain damage.

Two weeks after the surgery, staff removed the staples from his incision.

48

Advanced neuroimaging may have been met with reserved optimism from some scientists and philosophers, but a small group of literary scholars were much more enthusiastic. Here was a way, however limited, to match readers' mind states with their neural activity, empirical evidence for the brain on books.

Lisa Zunshine, who specializes in eighteenth-century fiction at the University of Kentucky, was an early cognitive critic. She suggests we are all greedy mind readers. What was an important evolutionary skill has become an insatiable need, and we read fiction – even narrative non-fiction, I'd argue – because, on some basic neural level, we do not distinguish between real people and people on the page. 'The very process of making sense of what we read,' she wrote in her 2006 treatise *Why We Read Fiction: Theory of Mind and the Novel*, 'appears to be grounded in our ability to invest the flimsy verbal constructions that we generously call "characters" with a potential for a variety of thoughts, feelings, and desires and then to look for the 'cues' that would allow us to guess at the feelings and thus predict their actions. Literature pervasively capitalizes on and stimulates Theory of Mind mechanisms that had evolved to deal with real people … '

49

I've read very few books written about fathers by their sons. Two of them, though – *The Scientists*, by Marco Roth, and Paul Auster's *The Invention of Solitude* – quote the same snippet from Kierkegaard: 'the one who works will give birth to his father.'

50

Saul and Nonni's first date was January 1958. His hairline already in retreat; his patter, I like to think, was snappy as his sport coat. He picked her up in a two-tone Dodge – beige and brown, with big fins – and took her to see Agatha Christie's *The Mousetrap*.

They were engaged three months later.

He was still living at home with his older brother, younger sister and their father. His mother had died four years earlier; a younger brother had already married and moved out. That spring, around the time of his engagement, the family sold their Grace Street house and moved to a new uptown bungalow on Park Home Avenue.

But six days a week he had to drive back downtown to his Adelaide Street office. He earned $400 each month; this would get bumped to $420 once he passed his final exam. He'd failed twice – the five-year chartered accountant correspondence course at Queen's University would take him seven years to complete.

He got the good news in the middle of his cousin's wedding. December, 1958. The newspaper used to publish the names of new graduates, so he and my mother ducked out of the reception to grab the late edition of the *Toronto Star*.

And there he was: Saul Akler, C.A.

I wonder: did he also check the racetrack results?

51

Wednesday, August 1: Blood test showed the level of his anti-scizure meds was actually too low, so they increased the dose. He has two blood clots in his right arm; one is superficial, the other, under the armpit, is called a deep vein thrombosis. Dr. Phan will consult with hematologist; if Saul's latest CT scan shows the bleeding on his brain has stabilized, they will approve a higher dose of blood thinner to prevent further clotting in his arm.

Thursday, August 2: Dr. Phan okayed an increase in blood thinner. Otherwise, no change.

Friday, August 3: No change.

Saturday, August 4: No change.

52

Bolt 9.63

The Summer Olympics were in London that year. The games were constantly showing on a large flat-screen TV in the CrCU lounge, an unwanted intrusion from the outside world. I arrived one Sunday, gave my name to the attendant behind the glass partition, who picked up the phone to the nurses' station. I glanced up at the TV. An official fired the starter's pistol and a group of sprinters shot out of the blocks, fifth among them the Jamaican Usain Bolt. He flashed past everyone and broke the 100-metre tape in 9.63 seconds. The attendant put down the phone. In the time it took for me to get buzzed in, I watched an Olympic-record run.

53

He is of the primal horde of sons who, as Freud liked to surmise, have it in them to nullify the father by force – who hate and fear him and, after overcoming him, honor him by devouring him.

This tasty bit of prose comes from *Patrimony*, by another Roth, the more famous Philip. Here, the author has taken a taxi to the University Hospital in New York City where his eighty-six-year-old father – who has been diagnosed with a brain tumour that's most likely benign – is recovering from a biopsy. En route, the cabbie somehow comes to believe that Roth is a psychiatrist and quickly offers up two common confessions: he's insecure and he hated his parents. Plus, a confession less common: the cabbie had actually punched his own father. Had knocked out the old man's four front teeth.

Roth, of course, notes the difference between himself and the bruiser behind the wheel: 'I'm from the horde that can't throw a punch. We aren't like that and we can't do it, to our fathers or to anyone else. We're the sons appalled by violence, with no capacity for inflicting physical pain, useless at beating and clubbing, unfit to pulverize even the most deserving enemy, though not necessarily without turbulence, temper, even ferocity. We have teeth as the cannibals do, but they are there, imbedded in our jaws, the better to help us articulate. When we lay waste, when we efface, it isn't with raging fists or ruthless schemes or insane sprawling violence but with our words, with our brains, with mentality … '

I read *Patrimony* that hot, suffocating August, the August of Saul's coma. After a forty-five-minute transit ride home from the hospital and a shower, I'd slump into a reclining deck chair and read. The book offered kinship, the comfort of the shared story. And even when that story was at its most mournful, I was not without solace.

Except for this section.

Because the cabbie had struck *me*, too. Punched his way off the page and rung my bell: was this character wholly imagined? He seemed too perfect, such a purely Rothian creation that the narrative abruptly lost all immediacy. I straightened up in my chair. Reread each word. Roth is well-known as a writer who turns himself inside out; his best fiction – *Deception*, *The Ghost Writer* – is stuffed with artfully rearranged biography, so why wouldn't his biography be similarly stuffed with fiction?

Patrimony, after all, has the provocative subtitle *A True Story*.

54

Saul had been unconscious for sixteen days. The longer he remained in a coma, the slighter the chance for full recovery. Even partial recuperation would be incremental, an agony. I sat at his bedside, did little but careen from cautious optimism to clear-eyed dread.

How thrilled I'd have been with even a small nod.

Meanwhile, a much more expansive drama was centred on another CICU patient. Hassan Rasouli was admitted to Sunnybrook two years earlier, October 2010. Doctors had successfully removed a benign brain tumour, but he developed bacterial meningitis, causing extensive brain damage. Rasouli was in a vegetative state for a month before the Sunnybrook team suggested he be removed from life support. The family – his wife, Parichehr Salasel; his daughter, Mojgan; and son, Mehran – refused. This type of end-of-life dispute is usually resolved at the Consent and Capacity Board, a provincially appointed body that has the legislative authority to decide such matters. The doctors, however, did not apply to the Board; they argued that Rasouli had no hope of recovery and it was the medically prudent choice to remove the ventilator. The fight went all the way up the legal ladder. The Superior Court of Ontario, the Ontario Court of Appeal and the Supreme Court of Canada all ruled in favour of the family.

The Rasouli case progressed over three years. So did the man. As the legal battle went back and forth, the medical conclusion began to change. Rasouli had remained on life support in Sunnybrook the whole time. The diagnosis was persistent vegetative state. But the family noticed small, hopeful signs.

As reported in *Toronto Life*: 'His wife claimed he could stick out his tongue on command. His eyes seemed to follow his family members around the room. In the summer of 2011, the family recorded video of Rasouli in bed. When Mojgan spoke to him in Farsi, telling him to stick out his fingers, he laboriously flexed them – first giving the thumbs-up, then raising his forefinger, then his middle finger.'

The family learned about the research of Adrian Owen, who conveniently moved from England to Canada and now had a lab at the University of Western Ontario. Rasouli became a test subject and the results proved him to be not vegetative but minimally conscious.

Minimally conscious patients are aware, both of themselves and their environment. They have an ability to respond and communicate. However, this ability is so limited, so random and fleeting that it is easy to miss. And misdiagnose. Owen's team has speculated that nearly 40 percent of those deemed vegetative do, in fact, have some degree of consciousness.

Hassan Rasouli could give a thumbs-up. His eyes could track. His family would bring him a computer tablet so he could watch old movies. One of his favourites, according to *Toronto Life*, was a Persian version of the story of Samson. His daughter Mojgan described the 'new shape' of her father's life: 'Maybe he's not able to sing for me, but I can play those songs from the movies for him.'

55

Tuesday, August 7: Three weeks since surgery. EEG showed no seizures.

Wednesday, August 8: Tracheostomy was done. Otherwise, no changes.

Thursday, August 9: Saul had an MRI and while they were taking him to have it done, a staff member saw his eyes open. Ed was there in the evening and thought Saul was opening and closing his mouth as if to speak.

Friday, August 10: Dr. Phan said the MRI results show the brain swelling is going down, the blood is being reabsorbed and Saul's brain is shifting back into position. Dr. Phan says he sees nothing that could be causing the coma. He said he lifted Saul's eyelid and flashed a penlight and it seemed that his eye was tracking the light.

Saturday, August 11: A CICU doctor raised his voice to try to get Saul's attention but nothing happened.

Sunday, August 12: No changes.

Monday, August 13: Saul was taken off the ventilator at 8:30 a.m. and spent the day breathing on his own. He goes back on the ventilator overnight and tomorrow they'll try him off it for twenty-four hours. Saul opened his eyes two different times today – briefly and unprompted. When a nurse asked him to raise his thumb, Saul did.

56

Saul did. *He did something.* Performed an unequivocally conscious act: he raised his thumb at the nurse's request. After twenty-four straight days in a coma, he had started to wake up. And here, in my Mead memo book, are the two words I wrote on the day of this momentous change: *sputum bus.*

Neuro patients, for reasons I never understood, can produce particularly pungent secretions. The phlegm is truly foul. Despite the fact that their injuries originate in the head, the smell is deeply intestinal, regurgitant. This is what bubbled out of Saul's tracheostomy tube. Nurses constantly had to suction it clean. I had not been overly squeamish about bodily fluids – splatters of blood and urine were not infrequent – but on this day, a day that seemed so pivotal to his recovery, I leaned in to kiss my father goodnight and the stench of his sputum nearly made me vomit all over him.

And on the ride home, just as the bus turned off Bayview Avenue to go west on Davisville, I sneezed into my hands and the stink was still there. In my nostrils, on my fingers, in the air immediately around me. I remained in a pocket of nausea for the rest of the day.

57

In *A Conversation with My Father*, an ailing, elderly man implores his daughter, the narrator, to write a simple story, 'the kind de Maupassant wrote, or Chekhov … ' The daughter tries to oblige but her two attempts fall flat. This leads to an argument over literary propriety: which details should be omitted, which included. The narrator's love of the non-linear story is played off against the old man's desire for traditional plot. This, Grace Paley once admitted, was her most autobiographical work. She would often butt heads with her father, would try to explain to him the problem with stories: people who live on the page like to outwit their writers.

58

A simple thumbs-up started a month of gestures, observed and analyzed. He was unpredictable. Began to turn his head toward a familiar voice one day, only to stare vacantly the next. His blood pressure dropped, doctors filled him with fluids and he rallied enough to squeeze my mother's hand. He went off the ventilator, was moved out of CRCU and up to the fifth floor. He waved at us. But soon he developed an infection and was moved down a floor to an isolation room, where we visited in gowns and masks and gloves, and nothing he did distinguished himself from his previous comatose state. Then the antibiotics kicked in. He moved his mouth as if to speak. Back up to the fifth floor. He had horrible bed sores. I asked if he knew who I was and he nodded a small, seismic nod. More and more, he moved his mouth, but no words, not even a whisper, issued forth. I recalled his Grade 6 report card from Clinton Public School in which his teacher, Ms. L. Rickaby, noted that 'Saul talks too much' in class. Susan and my mother laughed. My father's limbs were so swollen from his steroid medication that doctors prescribed a diuretic. Excess fluid escaped though his pores. We towelled him dry but it didn't stop. His arms and legs continued to weep.

Monday, September 3: Nurses on D5 find it too demanding to keep up with Saul's need for suction, so he may be moved back to CRCU. When we arrived, Saul opened his eyes and seemed to look at us and try to speak. When Howie spoke to him Saul lifted his fingers in acknowledgement. He was moved to an Intensive Care room in B wing, fifth floor, so he'll have more nursing attention and they can monitor his secretions. Saul was more or less awake during our visit from 1 to 5:30 p.m. Once, a B5 nurse asked him to raise his right thumb and after a delay, he did. She asked him to move his feet and he did. When she asked if he felt any pain, he very slightly shook his head.

Tuesday, September 4: Seven weeks since surgery. Saul only opened his eyes a few times. Still very phlegmy. Regularly being suctioned.

Wednesday, September 5: Another quiet day.

Thursday, September 6: Very little movement. Less need for suction though.

Friday, Sept 7: Blood test showed his anti-seizure meds are again below therapeutic levels. Both Nonni and the nurse have seen his left arm and shoulders twitching. If these are seizures, it might explain why he has been so quiet this week. The nurse gave Saul a haircut.

60

For almost two weeks, he tried to speak. There were two impediments: he did not have enough strength to push the air through his larynx. And when he got stronger, his tracheostomy tube blocked that passage anyway. The air that was supposed to vibrate his vocal cords instead escaped out of the hole in his throat. Eventually, we learned to cover the tracheostomy hole with a sterile gauze pad. He mustered up all his force and, sixty-six days after surgery, his breath finally became words.

'Stretch my leg,' said Saul.

'A ... K,' he spelled. 'L ... E ... R.'

The next day he looked at my mother. 'Naomi,' he said, using her given name.

And a few days after that, 'How much is this costing?'

62

He could communicate, could follow simple instruction. He would ask for a Kleenex and wipe his nose. He did none of these things with any regularity – days would pass between a gesture or response – but he showed enough cognitive function that we hoped his improvement would continue.

'You fell,' I said.

He looked at me without expression.

'You were at home. Mom was with you. She called the ambulance.'

Still nothing.

'Do you remember?'

Slowly, a nod. Then, 'Yes.'

The seconds between his sentence and mine stretched like months. He asked for his watch though it was clear he had no notion of time.

Disorientation is common to those who emerge from a minimally conscious to a confusional state. So are severe impairments of attention and memory, nighttime restlessness, daytime drowsiness and delusions.

One afternoon, I arrived in his room with Susan and my mother and we saw him struggle with a nurse. She was trying to inject medication into his PICC line. Saul fought back. My mother stroked his forearm. Susan reassured him. I held his hand.

'It's okay, Such,' I said. 'It's just your meds.'

'She's setting me up,' he told us. He cocked his fist, though so weakly a dandelion could have dodged the blow.

I began to show him old photographs. Hoped the solid foundation of personal history would support the wobbly here-and-now. He was propped up in bed and asked for his glasses. Put them on slightly askew and stared hard at the pictures. They were upside-down. I gently turned them right side up and watched him concentrate on those long-dead: his mother, his father, his older brother. His dexterity was poor. He fumbled with each one. Stopped at one of my favourites: a profile of twenty-two-year-old Saul, seated on a barstool. He has argyle socks and wide lapels. His rambunctious hair rises toward the ceiling.

'Who's that?' I asked.

The answer lolled somewhere in the long silence.

'Me?' he said.

'I stole a gun,' he told my mother a few days later. 'Don't tell anyone.'

64

Friday, November 23: Saul has been vomiting up his food for several days. He is still on an IV drip but is no longer being fed. He is having gastric juices suctioned out of his stomach. Staff are concerned that his hemoglobin is low and he may need another transfusion. Saul is asleep 95 percent of the time but opens his eyes when staff comes to work on him. He does not respond to instructions.

Monday, November 26: Staff started to give Saul 10 cc of food every hour and he has tolerated it okay. Saul may have smiled at a staff member over the weekend. He had his eyes open today and was looking around the room. Howie thought he was 'seeing.' Saul also tried to speak but was too weak.

Tuesday, November 27: Eighteen weeks since surgery. He didn't have his eyes open.

Wednesday, November 28: Saul's breathing was very fast and the nurse called the Rapid Response team. They got his breathing under control and did a CT scan on his right arm and chest in case a blood clot has formed in his lungs. The nurse thinks there is fluid in his lungs because he has gone off the diuretic. Saul was also taken off blood thinners recently because there was some blood in his stomach. We can't keep track of what medications he is or isn't taking. Saul has his eyes open today but isn't tracking. When we squeeze his hand he squeezes back.

ne'er toilet

I remember the late afternoon when my mother and I left the hospital to grab an early dinner from Subway and eat at her house. I stopped mid-bite. The house had become *hers*. I had by this time accepted that my father would not return home but the singularity of that word still had the power to startle me.

The house was full of his absence. Before I left that night, I went to the toilet. Took a shit where he had shat. There was a book of crossword puzzles on the counter. I thought of how he spent his hours, searching for the right word. I smiled: just like me. He had filled in the answers for *Drummer Krupa* and *Candice Bergen's dad*, but had left blank the four-letter space for *poetic 'never.'*

Ne'er, I wrote.

66

He stayed drowsy through much of December. Offered only limited response to yes-or-no questions, to the slender pain of needles. He was more alert when he sat up. Sometimes he was even stable enough for a wheelchair. Two nurses were needed for this task: one to strap him into a harness and spot him, while the other operated a mechanical arm that lifted him out of bed and lowered him into the chair.

I watched the procedure one chilly winter afternoon. Saw his skinny useless legs dangle in the air and I sought analogy: he looked like he'd been plucked from an icy river by a search-and-rescue helicopter. His hospital gown was askew, his blank expression began to change. My mind huddled in metaphor rather than read his moist brown eyes.

Family and staff filled a small conference room on the fifth floor. With odd formality, each person around the table gave their name and relationship to the patient: Nicolas, surgeon; Nonni, wife; Julie, nurse practitioner. And on. Children, spouses, occupational therapist, grandchildren, dietician. It had been five months since the surgery and we heard a full recap, from initial diagnosis to the latest infection. From a medical standpoint, he was stable enough for transfer to a long-term care facility that could better manage his many needs. Neurologically, there was nothing more to be done at Sunnybrook. Dr. Phan's words were blunt, professional, gentle. He told us what we all knew: this was likely the extent of Saul's recovery. No matter how sturdy his constitution, Saul was too weak to fight off infection after infection. The time had come for the family to consider comfort measures, end-of-life choices. Until then, he would continue to shuffle through levels of consciousness – from asleep to alert, vacant to drowsy.

Permanently inconsistent, I scribbled in my notebook. Because I wrote in haste, with barely a glance, the letters are wide and loopy. They burst the lined decorum of the page.

67

I had been matter-of-fact through much of this ordeal. Immersed myself in the daily reports, hour-to-hour medical details so that the bigger picture sometimes blurred. But the meeting with Phan brought it all back into terrible focus. On the way home from the hospital, Susan and I grabbed dinner. Chewed this over. We strained for objectivity. He was not vegetative, according to strict definition, but that seemed more a semantic concern than anything else. My father was being fed through a tube, could barely snatch conversation. He was vacant, frail, dying.

'I wish he could have one more good day,' Susan said. 'So he could enjoy a meal, watch a movie and talk his Saul talk.'

That did it. I am not lachrymose by nature – I tend to collapse inward rather than seep out – but there, on the steps outside Fanny Chadwick's restaurant, I finally sobbed and sobbed and sobbed.

I visited him twice a week for the rest of his life. Would pull up a chair and sit for hours. My mother was always there and together we'd just stare at Saul. Much of the time, of course, he did nothing. It was exceedingly dull but it had become crucial for me to witness whatever I could. I needed to watch him fiddle absently with a face cloth. See him scratch his nose. Each action was outsized, not only as a clue to his state of mind, but also because of the urgency of my attention. For so long I thought I was concerned about my father's level of consciousness but, really, I was absorbed in my own.

Because the more I did nothing but sit and watch him do nothing, the less inert I actually was. It began slowly – with simple recall, the scenes that held promise – and then sped up so whatever came to mind was immediately assessed for the page. I considered word choice, tone, structure.

And I collected new information, dipping into pop neuro-science and cognitive philosophy. I was promiscuous in the library stacks and online, though always with an eye on favourite writers – Paley, Michaels, Schuyler – in order to stay true to my own semiology.

In my notebook, for example, is this from Gilbert Rogin: 'My life consists of arranging and rearranging mysteries. A happy life is one of consonance, not resolution.'

Or Elizabeth Hardwick: 'The book – a plaguing growth that does not itself grow, but attaches, hangs on, a tumorous companion made up of the deranged cells of learning, experience, thinking.'

69

Sobbed and sobbed and sobbed. The scene outside Fanny Chadwick's did not appear in the first draft of this book, nor the second. Both times Susan noted its absence. It was, after all, a vivid moment in our story and yet one I opted not to include until this final draft.

I appreciate understatement in prose. Acknowledge that emotion stuffed deep enough into a sentence can create furious equipoise, a telling tension between what is said and what is unsaid. I like generous white space, a tidy page.

Perhaps this is *my* patrimony?

I knew I had decided to write this book when I began to watch movies with him in mind. Would return home from the hospital or work and want to check out *Double Indemnity* again, or *The Asphalt Jungle*. My desire was suspect. I took from these old crime films not simply moments of my past – memories of old Saturday nights with Saul – but also suggestions for future scenes. All I had in my notebook so far were random jottings, redolent moments. I needed dialogue.

So I sat at my father's bedside and did my shtick. Acted out Edward G. Robinson as claims investigator Barton Keyes, who listened to the *little man* in his gut whenever something smelled fishy. Repeated for him the line of Sam Jaffe's criminal mastermind Doc Riedenschneider, who was nabbed by the cops at a roadhouse because he lingered too long over a pretty girl: 'We all work for our vice.'

I'd wheel him down the hospital corridor. On good days, he would wave at familiar faces around the nurses' station. Nod at doctors. He'd peer with obvious interest into the rooms of other patients, even at the supply shelves stacked with cartons of latex gloves and hand sanitizer. The D5 wing was a long rectangle, and after a lap or two we would stop at the TV lounge, where I would find a movie channel for him to watch. He seemed to follow an old war flick once. Another time, we came across a 1940s melodrama that starred an actor whose face I couldn't quite place.

'Is that Fredric March or Broderick Crawford?' I asked.

Saul squinted at the wide screen. I noticed the thoughtful furrow in his brow.

'Yes,' he said.

One day, Susan and I took him down to the lobby of the hospital. He had not been this far from a nurse or doctor for six months. He seemed keen to the bustle: visitors bearing flowers and patients eating pizza and cabbies grabbing coffees.

I leaned close to his ear. 'Isn't this better than watching TV?'

He offered half a smile. 'No,' he said.

72

Late in December, we met with a Sunnybrook social worker. Softly, she used the exact phrase Dr. Phan had used – we had likely seen the extent of Saul's recovery – and explained the process of transferring him to a complex continuing care bed at another facility. We chose Baycrest, which began downtown in 1918 as the Toronto Jewish Old Folks Home before moving uptown in 1954 as part of a new hospital. In the past two decades, it has evolved into a top research centre for cognitive neuroscience. More relevant to us: Baycrest was a fifteen-minute walk from the house my parents had shared for a half-century. It was as close as he'd get to going home.

Not that our routine changed much. My father in bed, my mother and I in chairs beside him. We had learned how to suction out his trach hole rather than wait for a nurse to do so. Baycrest was less hectic than Sunnybrook, so Saul was given scheduled baths, regular grooming. I never shaved him again.

73

People often ask if this book is hard to write.

'No harder than the last one,' I answer.

Glib but true: though these actual events – my father's deterioration and brain damage, his death – were horrible to experience, they are no more or less difficult to depict than any fiction. I have always struggled to compose the simplest sentences. This goes beyond mere diction; even the tiniest inkling of thought must be teased out of a particular combination of sounds. Meaning usually comes hard on the heels of cadence.

There's a line from William Gass that lurks somewhere in my memory. I scan several tables of contents, three of the books of his criticism I have read over the years. And there, in his essay, *The Book As a Container of Consciousness*, is the dictum of transformation: the ideal writer must replace his own complex awareness with its equivalent in words. The sentence that gets set most rightly down ' ... is a bit of mind-song and a fully animated body made of muscle movement, ink, and breath.'

74

I showed him another photo, a trick shot snapped by Daniel many years ago. I'm a teenager, in red sweatshirt and blue jeans. I stand on my parents' front lawn, hands out, palms up. Saul stands a good twenty feet behind me. Also in a red shirt, also with his hands out. The gimmick of perspective makes him seem doll-sized, small enough for me to balance effortlessly in one hand.

75

So what happens when I write myself into a corner? My sentences turn claustrophobic, twitchy. They lose whatever harmony they had of sound and thought and I respond to this suffocation with nothing more than a nerveless stare. For days, for weeks, I have submitted meekly to an exhausted expression.

And a photo of us, side by side in a booth at the Free Times Cafe, on College Street. I was in a T-shirt and tweed jacket, he wore a shirt with vertical stripes – lavender, mauve and burgundy. White Kleenex in the breast pocket. He was spreading his hands wide and I remember he said something about Kensington Market, just across the street from the cafe: how my great-grandparents on both sides of the family had lived there during the Market's Jewish heyday in the early twentieth century.

I also remember that we took a stroll that day, after we left the cafe: Susan and I, Nonni and Saul. We wandered past places long-standing and those long-gone. There was the Kiever Synagogue, with its Byzantine stair towers and geometric stained glass; the Leonard Athletic Club, once home to boxers Baby Yack and Sammy Luftspring; and the menswear main-stay, Tom's Place, where my parents offered to buy me a suit. While an old Jewish salesman measured my chest and inseam, Saul talked about the *schmatte* business. And later, beside the cashier, he told another man about the famous custom clothier Lou Myles, born Louis Cocomile, to an Italian family who lived just blocks from my father's house.

'He made suits for Sinatra, De Niro, ' Saul said. 'And John Gotti. He was buried in a Lou Myles suit.'

'Oh yeah?'

'What's your line of work?' Saul asked.

The man, in a fat pinstripe suit and lemon-coloured ascot, tapped the tape measure that hung around his neck. 'I'm a tailor,' he said.

'Wha?'

'A tailor.'

My father nodded. 'You look like a confidence man,' he said.

77

He improved, out of the blue, for one week in spring. His voice became strong, his intonation familiar. He spoke of the surgery as if recent; while unclear on the *when* of his situation, he certainly knew the *where*. He wanted out of the hospital, fast.

'Where are my pants?' he said.

'You can't go anywhere, Such,' I told him.

He looked at me. His mouth tightened.

I reached out. 'You need to get your strength back.'

He swatted at my hand. 'Get away from me.'

There followed seconds of an enormous silence and then his expression eased. His eyes flickered. He had forgotten what he'd said.

I, of course, still remember.

Another memory: my mother and I side by side in hard chairs. She pulled a word-puzzle magazine out of her bag. I heard the dry rub of an eraser on the page, then soft pencil scratch. Saul, propped up on three pillows, tilted slowly to the right. I straightened him up. He looked at me without recognition. The bone flap from his operation had sagged inward; he had an indentation in his forehead the size of a golf ball. His expression drooped in accord. Maybe two minutes passed, maybe twenty, and then with the tiniest flicker of engagement he began to work the hem of his bedsheet between thumb and forefinger. My mother and I watched, shifted, went back to what we were doing. She erased something else. I flipped through her newspaper and saw the Obama administration had announced a decade-long investment in neurological research. The Brain Research through Advancing Innovative Neurotechnologies (BRAIN) Initiative would provide $100 million in first-year funding, spread across federal agencies and private foundations, and was to be spent on new ways to monitor vast amounts of neural activity. The payoff would be a deeper, if not comprehensive, understanding of the human brain in action.

Could the easy question really be answered in ten years?

Before the BRAIN Initiative had even begun, neuroscientists had long worked to suss out the neural connectivity of simpler species. Currently, the only animal with a complete neural map is the worm *Caenorhabditis elegans*, with 302 neurons that make 7,000 connections. Next up is the Drosophila fly and its 135,000 neurons. Research on more complicated animals continues with the zebrafish, which has roughly one million neurons. The smallest known mammal, the Etruscan shrew, has over one million neurons in the cortex alone. The leap from shrew to human, from the identification and connection of one million neurons to those of eighty-five billion, is so great that the necessary technology doesn't even exist *in theory*.

'What's the sequence?' my father suddenly asked one day. And then, as if to mock our lack of understanding of all that synaptic connectivity, added: 'You don't know the sequence.'

More than one year after the Obama announcement, the BRAIN Initiative granted funding for fifty-eight research projects. These include the development of a wearable brain scanner and advances in optogenetics, which uses light to stimulate neural activity. It has already been used to encode false memories in mice.

Not in the stack of photos was a picture of me, aged one. I'm in a crib, on my back. I look up, Saul reaches down. He is thirty-nine, a father for the fourth time with another on the way. I looked everywhere for this photo – through drawers and boxes and envelopes, both at my place and my mother's. It never turned up. Maybe I was mistaken, maybe it never did exist. But it remains an early, vivid memory: Hobby Horse wallpaper, dog-and-cat crib sheet. I'm in a yellow sleeper. Same smile as some of my maternal ancestors. Saul smiles too. His hair is dark and cut short. His glasses have thick frames. He wears a burgundy polo shirt with a mechanical pencil in the pocket. He leans his right elbow on the top bar of the crib and extends his left hand toward me just before the picture is snapped.

I was forty-four when Susan became pregnant. We told no one through the first trimester but him.

'I know you can keep a secret,' I said.

80

'What kind of an emotion is the desire to write?' asks neurologist Alice W. Flaherty in *The Midnight Disease*, her study of compulsive writing and block. 'It is not a core emotion like joy or fear. Nor is it a biological drive in the sense that hunger or sexual desire is. But there are secondary emotions and secondary drives, made of a mixture of core emotions and drives, often in combination with certain beliefs. Secondary emotions include complicated states such as guilt, hope, and smugness. Secondary drives might include the urge to buy a house or to gamble. It is in this secondary category that the drive to write best fits.'

The movie opens with an extended tracking shot: a man enters the Los Angeles Police Department building. He strides down the hallway, turns a corner and locates the Homicide Division.

'I wanna report a murder,' says the man.

'Where was the murder committed?' the cop asks.

'San Francisco.'

'Who was murdered?'

'I was.'

And then we flash back.

My father liked to joke that his favourite film was *D.O.A.* because the hero is an accountant. Frank Bigelow, however, shares few attributes with the pencil-pusher set. Played with sweaty vigour by B-movie veteran Edmond O'Brien, Bigelow itches to escape the life he shares in a dull California desert town with his secretary-girlfriend. He takes a solo getaway to San Francisco. Ogles girls. Gets himself poisoned. During a wild night at a jazz club, somebody slips a 'luminous toxin' into his whisky glass. The motive is ridiculous, contrived, pointless; nonetheless, the hero is doomed. What else can he do? He decides to make sense of what happened to him, to solve his own murder. The accountant becomes a detective.

The liveliest moments in *D.O.A.* come just after Bigelow learns he has days to live. He hears the doctor's words – 'nothing we can do' – but refuses to believe the diagnosis. He goes berserk. Runs wild through the streets of San Francisco before stopping, breathless, beside a newsstand on Embarcadero. *LIFE* magazine is clearly visible behind him. According to film historian Jack Shadoian, the 'great shots of Bigelow running madly through the crowded streets and traffic, done in a series of wipes, are unforgettably nightmarish. His run is the expression of what he feels, but he runs through an actual environment, not a phantasmagorical one. The setting vibrates with an unscoured fidelity; people stop and stare at this man running at top speed, pushing them aside, heedlessly plunging into traffic – and then go on their way.'

The story goes that director Rudolph Maté did not have official permission for a street shoot. But he did it anyway. So all those people who stop and stare are not actors at all; they are real pedestrians. They *are* actually being shoved aside by O'Brien, playing Bigelow. The questions on their faces are pure and unmediated. The scene never fails to captivate me. I can watch it over and over.

82

He was riled up during our final exchange. I came for a visit and found him once again struggling with a nurse. She held a syringe in one hand and fended him off with the other.

'Please, Mr. Akler,' she said.

'I'm on to you,' my father said.

I pinned down his wrists. He continued to act up.

'It's what they always give you, Dad. Same thing every day.'

'That's what you want me to think.'

Nothing could soothe him save his own lack of stamina. He ran out of fight seconds later. I felt his spindly forearm muscles twitch in my grip. I took a deep breath.

83

11:06

The call came as I sipped a coffee. My mother reported on his bowel constriction, low blood pressure. Saul was being sent to the emergency room at North York General.

'It doesn't look good,' she said.

I knocked back my espresso. Rinsed out the demitasse. Susan started to cancel her plans for the day, but I was casual about the news, offhand. Dire situations had become the norm. I walked, alone and without urgency, to the subway. Transferred from the eastbound Bloor line to Yonge, went north, and was unperturbed by a four-minute delay at Eglinton. I hit the Sheppard subway line and went east again to Leslie station and arrived at the hospital, in no great rush, eight minutes too late.

The one pure fact in my Mead memo notebook consists not of words but numbers. 11:06. The exact time of his death.

I have a copy of my father's Patient Care Notes, sent along with him from Baycrest to North York General that day:

> *Meningioma right frontal. Resection July 2012. Collapse of mesh.*
>
> *Seizure disorder, non-convulsive. Stable on slightly subtherapeutic levels.*
>
> *Hypertension*
>
> *Dyslipidemia*
>
> *Cognitive impairment: gradual decline × 3 years*
>
> *Sacral wound – healing well but slowly. Adhesive dermatitis. Wash out wound and layer Inandine to base with each bowel movement*
>
> *Ulcerative colitis – 2–4 loose stools/day*
>
> *Depression*

Doctors never mentioned anything to us about depression. And yet, in all his bedridden months, could there have been any surer sign that he was aware?

Consciousness is recursive. I sit in a chair now and try to write about when I sat in a chair then. This resists easy narrative. Sections of this book are more associative, like thought, rather than linear, like narrative. Yet I have imposed numbers on each. A futile attempt to adduce experience. No matter how I shuffle cold fact, near-faithful reminiscence, cognitive and literary tidbit, I cannot get close enough. I am doomed to revision.

86

Whenever I wrote these words – during his coma, or immediately following the funeral, or long after – I was always fully aware of my need to reshape each moment, to mediate between lived experience and polished expression; so much so that my mind often moved ahead of an event. I would imagine some poignant exchange and wait dumbly for it to unfold.

On no day did this seem more bathetic than November 6, 2014 – the one-year anniversary of my father's death. I envisioned the scene weeks in advance: my mother and I at the cemetery, bare trees, subdued light. We would both hold a small stone retrieved by my brother from the bank of the Ganges – she keeps a bag of them in her car – and then, one after the other, place them on the headstone. I would take a step back and study the nine chiselled letters that comprised his name, blink once, twice, then start to talk about, say, the TV remote.

'Remember it died the day of his funeral?'

My mother would nod.

'Like a dog lying down on his master's grave.'

The day at the cemetery never did happen. Bad weather, a change of plans. But the bit about the TV remote is still true.

87

The last thing he wrote, in a weak, spidery hand: *Can't you speak louder?*

The best writing has a resonance beyond literal meaning. When I put pen to paper I approach some unnamed need, a jumble of emotion and thought that could not otherwise be parsed. I want the right words in the right order. I want to straddle, in Alice Flaherty's words, the dictionary and the scream.

I had the baby strapped to my chest. She was seven months old. I walked her for two hours up and down a dead-end dirt road in Prince Edward County. Hazel was born twenty-eight days after Saul died. We expected the timing to be even tighter – the baby had dropped into the birth position two weeks before his death. Susan and I tried to prepare for the possibility that she could go into labour during the funeral. I shrugged off this memory, such bad fiction. I maintained my pace. Pebbles rolled underfoot. I could hear the baby's breathing soften. She began to snooze. I moved some sentences around in my head.

Notes and Acknowledgements

Quotations and references are from, in order of appearance:

p. 13: Sven Birkerts, 'The Art of Attention,' *Aeon* magazine, 24 May 2013.

p. 22: Leonard Michaels, 'Masks and Lies,' *The Essays of Leonard Michaels*, 2009.

p. 25: Daniel Dennett, *Intuition Pumps and Other Tools for Thinking*, 2013.

p. 31: Lyndall Gordon, *Lives Like Loaded Guns: Emily Dickinson and Her Family's Feuds*, 2010.

p. 35: Daniel Dennett, *Consciousness Explained*, 1991.

p. 36: Larissa Macfarquhar, 'Two Heads,' *New Yorker*, 12 February 2007.

p. 40: Peter C. Whybrow, *A Mood Apart*, 1997.

p. 43-44: Joung H. Lee, ed., *Meningiomas: Diagnosis, Treatment, and Outcome*, 2008.

pp. 44-45: Michael Bliss, *Harvey Cushing: A Life in Surgery*, 2005.

p. 49-50: Wilder Penfield, 'Some Mechanisms of Consciousness Discovered During Electrical Stimulation of the Brain,' *Proceedings of the National Academy of Sciences*, 15 February 1958.

p. 51: Birkhard Bilger, 'The Possibilian,' *New Yorker*, 25 April 2011

p. 54: 'Why Genre Matters: Dinah Lenney interviews Judith Kitchen, David Biespiel, Scott Nadelson and Sven Birkerts,' *Los Angeles Review of Books*, 23 August 2013.

p. 58: James Schuyler, 'Pastime,' from *Selected Poems*, 1970.

p. 64, 66: Michael S.A. Graziano, 'Are we really conscious?,' *The New York Times*, 10 October 2014.

p. 72: Kat McGowan, 'Rediscovering Consciousness in People Diagnosed as "Vegetative,"' *Discover*, March 2011.

p. 75: Lisa Zunshine, *Why We Read Fiction: Theory of Mind and the Novel*, 2006.

p. 80: Philip Roth, *Patrimony*, 1991.

pp. 82–83: Nicholas Hune-Brown, 'A Life Interrupted,' *Toronto Life*, November 2012.

p. 86: Grace Paley, 'A Conversation with My Father,' *Enormous Changes At the Last Minute*, 1974.

p. 98: Gilbert Rogin, *What Happens Next?*, 1971.

p. 98: Elizabeth Hardwick, *Sleepless Nights*, 1979.

p. 103: William H. Gass, 'The Book As a Container of Consciousness,' *Finding a Form*, 1996.

p. 111: Alice W. Flaherty, *The Midnight Disease: The Drive to Write, Writer's Block, and the Creative Brain*, 2004.

My mother, Nonni Akler, has been a source of kindness and strength during my father's life and after. She patiently endured my many questions and invasions of her privacy. So too, my siblings – Trudy, Daniel, Matt and Ed. This is my version of our story.

Special thanks to Derek McCormack and Adam Sternbergh, both of whom made important contributions to the text.

Deep gratitude to everyone at Coach House Books. To Jason McBride and Alana Wilcox: I am lucky that two of the sharpest minds in the business happen to belong to two of my closest friends.

To Susan Kernohan, whose presence is everywhere in this book and out.

And to Hazel Akler, future reader.

About the Author

Howard Akler is the author of *The City Man* (2005), which was nominated for the Amazon First Novel Award, the City of Toronto Book Award and the Commonwealth Writers' Prize. He lives in Toronto.

About the
Exploded Views Series

Exploded Views is a series of probing,
provocative essays that offer surprising
perspectives on the most intriguing
cultural issues and figures of our day.
Longer than a typical magazine article
but shorter than a full-length book,
these are punchy salvos written by some
of North America's most lyrical journal-
ists and critics. Spanning a variety of
forms and genres – history, biography,
polemic, commentary – and published
simultaneously in all digital formats and
handsome, collectible print editions,
this is literary reportage that at once
investigates, illuminates and intervenes.

www.chbooks.com/explodedviews

Typeset in Goodchild Pro and Gibson Pro. Goodchild was designed by Nick Shinn in 2002 at his ShinnType foundry in Orangeville, Ontario. Shinn's design takes its inspiration from French printer Nicholas Jenson who, at the height of the Renaissance in Venice, used the basic Carolingian minuscule calligraphic hand and classic roman inscriptional capitals to arrive at a typeface that produced a clear and even texture that most literate Europeans could read. Shinn's design captures the calligraphic feel of Jensen's early types in a more refined digital format. Gibson was designed by Rod McDonald in honour of John Gibson FGDC (1928–2011), Rod's long-time friend and one of the founders of the Society of Graphic Designers of Canada. It was McDonald's intention to design a solid, contemporary and affordable sans serif face.

Printed at the old Coach House on bpNichol Lane in Toronto, Ontario, on Rolland Opaque Natural paper, which was manufactured, acid-free, in Saint-Jérôme, Quebec, from 50 percent recycled paper, and it was printed with vegetable-based ink on a 1965 Heidelberg KORD offset litho press. Its pages were folded on a Baumfolder, gathered by hand, bound on a Sulby Auto-Minabinda and trimmed on a Polar single-knife cutter.

Series editor: Jason McBride
Cover by Ingrid Paulson
Author photo by Susan Kernohan

Coach House Books
80 bpNichol Lane
Toronto ON M5S 3J4
Canada

416 979 2217
800 367 6360

mail@chbooks.com
www.chbooks.com